Storystarters

200+ Writing Prompts
That Lead To Stories

By Rob Bignell

Atiswinic Press · Ojai, Calif.

STORYSTARTERS
200+ WRITING PROMPTS THAT LEAD TO STORIES

A GUIDEBOOK IN THE STORYTELLING 101 SERIES

Copyright Rob Bignell, 2016

Atiswinic Press
Ojai, Calif. 93023
https://inventingrealityediting.wordpress.com/home

ISBN 978-0-9961625-5-5

Cover design by Rob Bignell
About the Author photo by Bryan Bignell

Manufactured in the United States of America
First printing July 2016

For Kieran
My favorite future
storyteller...

Contents

INTRODUCTION   1

WRITING PROMPTS   9
Acceptance   11
Aging   13
Ambition   15
Avoidance   16
Betrayal   18
Confusion   20
Control   21
Deceit   23
Distrust   25
Doubt   27
Dreams   29
Experimentation   31
Fear   33
Finding meaning   35
Guilt   37
Hope   39
Identity   40
Inflexibility   41
Innocence lost   42
Isolation   44
Jealousy   46
Loneliness   48
Loss   49
Manipulation   50

Masquerade   52
Memory   54
Misconception   55
Mysterious gift   57
Obsession   58
Out of one's league   59
Perfection   60
Promise   62
Race   64
Reclaim   65
Removal   67
Resistance   69
Returning   70
Revenge   71
Sanity   73
Secrecy   74
Separation   75
Tracked   77
Trapped   78
Turning a new page   79
Uncertainty   81
Vengeance   83
Violence   85
Wrongly accused   87
Zealotry   88

CREATE YOUR OWN PROMPTS   89

Introduction

Among the greatest challenges facing writers is coming up with and developing a fantastic story idea. The problem isn't that writers have a shortage of ideas, just that many concepts are not very good, as currently formulated in their head. They sense that and so sometimes face a mini-episode of writer's block.

Being proactive, they turn to writing prompts – a single word, a phrase, a situation, or a picture – to spur their imagination, to inspire them. Often, writers find that while these prompts result in a lot of creative output, they still don't result in a story that is publishable.

Why that is seems confusing. Our teachers from grade school through high school, maybe even in college, gave out writing prompts that almost always led to a flurry of words and a feeling of success. Sometimes our teachers' positive response to what was written spurred us to write with even more vigor.

Recently while looking back at my own school-generated juvenilia for story ideas, I found it was unusable, not because it was bad (okay, it was bad though rescuable) but because it was based on pointless writing prompts – *While digging in your backyard, you find a large box. What's in the box?* or *You're the first person to step foot on Mars. What do you see or experience?*

Such prompts almost never lead to an actual story, as the prompt does not focus on what a story is about: resolving a conflict.

Conflict: The heart of every story

When telling a story, you've got to have conflict in it. If there's no conflict, you have a wooden story that starts nowhere, leads nowhere, and ends nowhere. As E.M. Forster noted, "'The king died, then the queen died' is a plot. 'The king died, then the queen died of grief' is a story."

Forster's quotation is apt because a good story is about at least one character under adversity. Conflict typically arises from the characters' perceptions, needs and wants. As each character has an urgent personal agenda, your plot really is a synthesis of its individual characters' efforts to achieve their agendas. Hence, Odysseus must get home, but the gods don't want him to. Hamlet must be absolutely certain his uncle killed the king, but self-doubt gets in his way. Luke Skywalker must save a princess, but stormtroopers are after him. Those are stories.

Suppose we are reading a story about Nazi-occupied France. The agenda of our hero, British secret agent Captain Smith, is to persuade French villagers to form a resistance cell so that the community may be used as a base of operations against the Nazis. The agenda of our villain, Army Hauptmann Müller, is to occupy the village and surrounding countryside so that France may be used as a base of operations against the British Isles. The villagers' goal is to stay neutral; they don't like the Nazis but fear their wrath.

As these conflicting agendas intersect, each character faces adversity. For Smith, the villagers aren't receptive to his idea perhaps Müller ultimately is captures him. For Müller, smith blows up an ammunition dump, and then the villagers are uncooperative when Smith escapes his cell. For the villagers, they first feel the pressure of Smith and Müller and then watch both sides become increasingly violent toward one another on their home turf.

There are five primary types of conflict that your characters can face:

• **Man vs. nature** – When the forces of nature, such as storms, deserts and volcanoes, that hinder a character from achieving his objective

• **Man vs. man** – When two individuals struggle against one another to achieve their objectives, such as Smith and Müller

• **Man vs. society** – When a character or small group challenges the mores and values of their culture or its political institutions

• **Man vs. God(s)** – When an individual or a small group fight God or the gods

• **Man vs. himself** – When a character has an internal struggle because of conflicting desires, wants and needs

The prompts mentioned on pp. 1-2 easily could have led to stories if only they were restructured so that they focused on conflict. For example, *While digging in your backyard, you find a small box containing your mother's diary, which reveals the dad who raised you really isn't your father. How do you go about determining the truth? How does this alter your perception of your parents? How do you find peace with your parents and yourself at this news?* Or *Your ship crashes on Mars so that you have no way to return home. How do you survive until a rescue can be mounted?*

As reading through books on writing prompts, I found most were useless for anything beyond journaling or introducing students to certain modes of writing, such as descriptive writing or character building. To generate a story, a new approach to writing prompts was needed. Thus was born this book.

How to build a story from a writing prompt

Each of the prompts listed in this book center on a conflict. You can use them to build either a short story or a novel.

The first step in doing so is to **select one from the list**. Pick the prompt that inspires your creativity, that starts your imagination running in all kinds of directions about how such a tale might be written. Let's suppose, for the sake of example, that you choose this prompt: *The main character, dealing with personal guilt for a bad, injurious choice he once made, finds a victim of a crime paralleling his. The discovery of this victim makes his guilt so unbearable that he must atone for it to set his world right. How does he go about coping with* *his guilt and making it right so he can live with himself?*

The next step is to **give your prompt a setting**, a place and time for the conflict to unfold. After all, the ways our main character attempts to solve his problem always occur within the context of the setting. For example, if in the opening of the story a man finds a dead child, left in a garbage bag in a trash container, the setting might be his run-down apartment complex and the morning when he takes out his garbage before heading to work.

After establishing the setting, **devise ways the main character might solve the prompt's central problem**, in this case coping with his guilt and making it right so he can live with himself.

To do that, you might spend some time determining what the main character feels guilty about. Perhaps a decade before he was a sergeant in the Army, serving in Afghanistan, and one of the village's mothers came to him for help because the local chieftain was physically and sexually abusing her son. He is ordered not to get involved in local affairs, however, and a few days later fellow soldiers find the boy's dead, broken body left in the village refuse dump. Our main character feels that his inaction led to the boy's death.

So how does he atone for his guilt? Perhaps, after seeing the current murdered child's mother on the news and after an interviewing police detective tells him not to get involved any further, he decides to solve the crime. Along the way, he realizes he's out of his realm and that perhaps, if he cannot solve the crime, he must bury his guilt again. Maybe he seeks solace in someone – say a family member or a priest. There are thousands of directions to take the story, and you'll need to go the route that best fits what you're familiar with and the message you want to convey (For example, solving the crime means you have a mystery or an action-adventure tale; confessing to a priest might carry a spiritual theme). Regardless of which path is taken, you now have a loose outline of the story.

From there, **fill in the details of the outline**, **start writing**, or **create dossier of your characters**. No matter your preferred method, you're on your way to writing a story rather than an unusable (albeit delightful to pen) passage that results from your standard fare writing prompt, such as *What is the weather like at someplace you wish you could be* or *write about a ship that can take you places you've never been before.*

How this book is organized

Prompts in this book are organized alphabetically by a word that describes the motivation or event that leads to a conflict. They are then divided by the type of conflict (man vs. man, man vs. himself, etc.).

Of course, there can be some crossover between the motivations and events. When isn't betrayal a form of deceit, after all? Betrayal isn't the only kind of deceit, of course, just as a square isn't the only kind of rectangle. Given this, the entries in this volume hyperfocus on the keyword; for example, betrayal is the only kind of deceit under the *betrayal* entry. Further, a more general keyword, such as *deceit*, doesn't include those story conflicts that could be construed as a subtype – such as *betrayal* – when that more specific word appears in the volume.

In addition, often multiple conflicts appear in any given story. Consider a man vs. nature story, in which the protagonist must overcome the challenges a desert environment throws at him: the unrelenting heat; the blinding sun; the lack of water for miles. Along the way, the protagonist almost certainly will face a man vs. himself conflict in which he doubts if he can go on as mocking vultures circle overhead. There probably are other conflicts as well; perhaps a man vs. man conflict between the protagonist and the antagonist occurred when the latter betrayed our main character by abandoning him in this inhospitable environment.

Given this, the entries that follow in this guide often will include more than one conflict, especially in the man vs. nature offerings. Most often the additional conflict is of the man vs. himself variety. Such a conflict can add depth and sophistication to your story.

One last note: For style purposes, all of the prompts are written as if the character were a male, but they just as easily could be a woman. No slight is intended.

All right, let's get started!

Writing Prompts

T he following 200+ writing prompts are divided by topic. Each topic in turn has four prompts that fit into the various categories of conflicts that might appear in a story. Sometimes there is crossover – a man vs. man conflict might be included in a man vs. nature prompt, for example – but remember that rarely does a story contain only one kind of conflict.

Acceptance

Man vs. nature

To gain acceptance in society, a young man must prove himself by surviving in the wilderness via some sort of rite of passage. What does the main character learn about himself – and about his society's values – as he overcomes the dangerous challenges that nature throws at him during this rite?

Man vs. man

A son seeks the acceptance of his father or a daughter of her mother. Why does the parent not accept the child for who he is? Why does our protagonist now feel he needs to – and is able to – gain acceptance (Perhaps the parent is terminally ill, so there is a ticking clock.)? How does the child go about seeking this acceptance, and why is the parent still resistant to giving it?

Man vs. society

Our protagonist – an outsider – must find a way to fit into his school/workplace/church/town. When he learns a secret that could make him the hero, however, no one believes him. How does he prove his secret to them? Given their attitude toward him, why does he simply not keep the secret to himself and let them suffer the consequences of not knowing the truth until it's too late?

Man vs. himself

Unable to get along socially in an environment from

which he cannot leave, our main character must decide
if he should change himself – that is not be true to himself – to fit in or if he should accept alienation as his lot
and make due. Or is there a third option for our main
character?

Aging

Man vs. nature

Our protagonist, now retired, decides to move back to the place of his childhood and renovate an old residence that nature is quickly reclaiming. As he struggles against the damage that Mother Nature has wrought (pipes broken from overgrown roots, weeds, rotted roof that leaks, etc.), how does he come to terms with his own aging, which is ravaging his once virile body?

Man vs. man

The main character, near the end of his life, is on the verge of achieving his life-long dream – but one person, a lifelong nemesis – stands in his way. How does the main character overcome his nemesis? What is the dream our main character seeks (perhaps it is a metaphor for some idea or concept)? Why does he believe achievement of this dream matters more than anything else?

Man vs. society

A man who is an expert on a problem society faces is brought out of retirement to advise a force sent to cope with this challenge – but the way he conducts himself clashes with the unit of young men who, focused on the present, know too little of the past and who he really is. How does he overcome ageism and advise – and maybe eventually lead – the force to victory?

Man vs. himself

Our main character finds that an old flame from his younger days wants to rekindle their relationship, despite that he has built a life with another woman and has children. What would compel him to consider experiencing this love from his past? What happens if he dips into this forbidden love only to have the undertow pull him in?

Ambition

Man vs. nature

A man faces the challenge of crossing a desert on foot. Why does he need to cross it? What obstacles will he face on the way?

Man vs. man

Two men possess the same goal. Why do they each have that ambition? What is at stake for each man if they do not achieve their goal? What tussles have they had in the past with one another that causes them to dislike the other (and hence turns up the desire for each to achieve their goal)?

Man vs. society

What happens when a man's ambitions run against his society's values? In what ways are society's values questionable (so that the reader will root for the main character)?

Man vs. himself

A man must decide if his ambition is worth pursuing. What external and internal forces tug at him to continue the pursuit, as well as to quit? What is the price of pursuing and of giving up on his ambition?

Avoidance

Man vs. nature

On an important journey – perhaps to deliver a message, person or item – the main character hopes to avoid a naturally perilous area, such as a treacherous mountain range or an expansive badlands, due to its inhospitable conditions and dangerous animals and plants. Unfortunately for the main character, to complete his journey, he is forced to cross this area he hopes to avoid. How does he survive it? What virtues does he possess that allows him to survive? What lessons does he learn during his efforts?

Man vs. man

What if two people who don't like one another are forced to live together? Perhaps it's a married couple that has split, with one living upstairs and the other in the basement, or maybe it's a stepparent and a teenage stepchild. How do the two avoid one another? What event must and internal changes in their thinking must occur to bring them together?

Man vs. society

Your main character witnesses something illegal. The power behind the illegal activity wants to shut up your main character before he reveals what he knows – except nobody believes him (unbeknown to the group behind the illegal activity) and he must search for more evidence to prove his claim so he may get the protection and help he needs.

Man vs. himself

To stay alive, the main character must defeat an evil character. The main character soon realizes, however, that to do this, he symbolically must make a bargain with the devil, something he hoped to avoid. What moral debates goes through his head as deciding whether or not to accept the bargain?

Betrayal

Man vs. nature

A man who should have been hailed as a hero is betrayed and left to die in an unforgiving environment. How does he survive the obstacles nature throws at him? As overcoming these hurdles, what skills or knowledge does he gain that allows him to either thrive there or upon reaching his homeland to return his status to that of a hero?

Man vs. man

What if our protagonist's best friend betrays him? How does our main character cope with this realization? How does he set things straight – perhaps such as revenge or redoubling his efforts to achieve his goals despite the betrayal?

Man vs. society

Our main character discovers that several people in her organization (business, political office, etc.) who are in his employ have betrayed him. Firing those people isn't enough, though, for they've tied up the organization in deals and secrets that will cause his fall and financial ruin. How does he unravel the truth behind these betrayals and right her ship before it sinks?

Man vs. himself

To achieve an important objective that will save a number of people, the main character must betray those who are closest to him – perhaps his family, perhaps an organization he belongs to. What inner struggles does the character go through to decide if he should commit this betrayal? Do the needs of the many truly outweigh the needs of the few – even if those few mean more to the main character than anyone else?

Confusion

Man vs. nature

Your main character wakes up in an unknown location and is confused about how he got there. How does he go about determining where he is? How does he get home? And how did he end up at that location?

Man vs. man

The main character discovers a mysterious structure. What threat does it pose to the main character and others? How was it discovered? What secrets does it resist yielding? While not a human per se, the structure can be a character itself.

Man vs. society

A missing person from a cold case suddenly shows up. Where was this person all these years? What if those responsible for his disappearance want to keep this information secret?

Man vs. himself

What happens when the main character discovers his father isn't the idol or paragon of virtue that the perspective of childhood led him to believe? How does this lead to confusion in the main character about his sense of identity? How does he find peace with the revelations about his father – and with himself?

Control

Man vs. nature

Our protagonist is marooned in an inhospitable environment. To survive, he attempts to control it but is met with disaster at every turn. What if to survive he must not control the environment but instead live in harmony with it? How does he come to this realization? How does this outlook affect his overall perspective on life?

Man vs. man

What if a successful man – one with a profitable business and who is popular – loses control to his emotions (perhaps his heart wins over his rationality or he tries some addictive drug) for a single night and in doing so jeopardizes all he's built? How does he regain control of himself despite the lure of the person who helped/caused him to give in to his emotions? Or does he decide to give up "control" (and if so, why)?

Man vs. society

To survive, a society must naturally limit some individual freedoms. What happens, though, in situations where a main character believes those limits are oppressive? What would the main character do to regain some control over his life?

Man vs. himself

Our protagonist loses his job, suffers a divorce, and finds himself cut off from his friends and family all within a few months time. How does he cope with this

downward spiral in his life and the self-doubt that ac-
companies it? Can he regain control of his life – or is
such control merely a myth?

Deceit

Man vs. nature

While in the wilderness, a man finds himself engaged in a chess-like match with a long-time rival who wants him dead. Why are they rivals? Forced to utilize the materials in their surroundings, which one can employ the right amount of misdirection to overcome the other?

Man vs. man

What if our main character realizes he's a pawn in someone's game, being manipulated to serve that person's ends? What is the manipulator's goal and why would he choose our protagonist for this role? How does the main character turn the tables on the manipulator?

Man vs. society

An organization frames our main character. How does he elude authorities as finding proof of his innocence? Why did this organization set up our main character? That is, was he just an expendable fall guy or something more?

Man vs. himself

Given the opportunity of a lifetime, a man is asked to ghostwrite for a famous author. But when the man sees his words only bring more fame and respect to the author, he begins to wonder if he can carry on this deceit. Do the riches the author lavishes upon our main character outweigh self-pride's demands that he be recognized for his talents?

Distrust

Man vs. nature

The power goes out, and a group of people in a some-what isolated location find themselves at the mercy of nature and unable to communicate with the outside world. Thanks to misinterpretation and doubt, they soon find themselves unable to trust one another. Can they overcome the wild possibilities offered up by a few frightening facts to work together so they can overcome the dangers nature tosses at them?

Man vs. man

What if two brothers who deeply hate one another must come together to stop a threat that endangers something they mutually love? How did the brothers come to dislike one another? What skill does each possess that makes their cooperation necessary to defeat this threat? How are they ever able to work together?

Man vs. society

Our main character finds himself in a place where friends are indistinguishable from enemies. What would be such a location in our society (A war zone? A workplace full of interoffice politics?)? How does he weave his way through and out of such a place?

Man vs. himself

The protagonist is a victim of a crime in a community he's moved to and because of it loses his sense of security there. How does he keep this fear from becoming a neurosis, and how does he regain trust of others in his new hometown?

Doubt

Man vs. man

Our protagonist is tapped to help a powerful, secret organization solve a major problem. A man from the organization – who he is assigned to work with – has serious doubts about the protagonist's abilities and chances of success, however. How does the protagonist overcome this adversity so he can solve the problem? What special skill or knowledge does the protagonist possess that makes him indispensable? Why would the man from the organization doubt our protagonist?

Man vs. society

The main character decides the organization he works for is stepping over the line despite its noble goals. How does he come to this decision? How does the organization deal with his objections?

Man vs. God(s)

What if a man who doubts God's existence still lives in fear of actually having been made in God's image? That is, he may not be God-fearing, but he is God-haunted. Why does he harbor doubts about God? How does balancing his doubt with his fear affect him, and how does he rectify the two?

Man vs. himself

Our main character possesses serious self-doubt about his artistic abilities (as a painter, a musician, a sculptor, etc.) yet is unable to give up on his passion (for doing so means giving up on himself). How does he deal with his self-doubt so that he can actually create? Is his self-doubt, ironically, what propels him to create truly great pieces that show he actually has superior artistic abilities?

Dreams

Man vs. nature

Our main character, an average bloke, resolves to achieve some great physical feat, perhaps climbing a mountain. What motivates him to actually fulfill this dream? Why does he dream of accomplishing this specific challenge? What obstacles does he face in actually fulfilling this dream or as making the climb?

Man vs. man

The protagonist faces a difficult decision: Should he help make happy the person he most loves by breaking his own heart? Why does our protagonist love this person? How does he try to get this person to be happy without breaking his heart?

Man vs. society

What if our main character learns that to achieve his dream he must despoil something? Why would he care about this something? How do others in his corporation/military unit/family encourage him to pursue his dream despite this despoiling? How does our main character come to decide his dream is not worth the price?

Man vs. himself

What if the main character, who has the opportunity to realize his dream of going someplace or holding a certain position, must leave behind his fragile mother or father to do so? Which would he choose and what would be the thoughts he'd have along the way in making this decision?

Experimentation

Man vs. nature

What if when undergoing an experiment to cure some terminal disease, the treatment has an unintended consequence? How does this physically and psychologically affect our protagonist? What if he seeks some way to overcome the consequence because he deems it being as bad as having the original disease?

Man vs. man

A man discovers he is part of a grand experiment that is kept secret from him and society at large. What is the experiment? Why does the man not want to be part of it and plans to escape from and makes public the experiment? What if another man is sent to kill our main character before he can? How does our hero outwit this antagonist and survive?

Man vs. society

What if an organization wants our main character to conduct an experiment that he believes is unethical? What is the experiment and the possible gains to be had from it? How does our main character try to avoid running the experiment?

Man vs. himself

A person bored with his life decides to experiment. While at first exhilarating, the need for ever-riskier experimentation leads him on a deep, downward spiral. How does the main character deceive himself to believe that the experimentation is not destroying his life? How does he find a way to reverse his course and bring excitement to his life without dangerous experimentation, or will his life end tragically?

Fear

Man vs. nature

Our main character is placed in an environment that he has a great fear of. Perhaps it's a jungle where he's afraid of snakes or a yacht where he's afraid of the ocean. Why does he have this fear? When a threatening situation arises (plane crashes in jungle, yacht stuck in a tropical storm), how does he survive these forces of nature, and how does he overcome his fear?

Man vs. man

A man discovers he's being spied on but has no idea why. Fearful of what might occur to him, he decides to learn why he is being followed, not through a direct confrontation but secretly, as he believes this is the only way to learn the truth. In doing so, he engages in a deadly cat and mouse game with the man spying on him.

Man vs. society

The main character introduces some act of social innovation and progress to a parochial conservative community. How do some community members oppose this progress? How do a few others accept and even come to advocate it, making the conservatives even more paranoid of the change?

Man vs. himself

Our main character hears strange noises in the night, but when he goes to investigate cannot determine what what they are. The noises continue, however. What if our main character comes to believe he is going insane? How does he arrive at this conclusion? What if the noises symbolize the emotions that lead him to doubt himself?

Finding meaning

Man vs. nature

Our main character, attempting to make his life rise above the mediocre, decides to go on a great adventure that tests and proves his mettle (think John Mayer's "Walt Grace's Submarine Test, January 1967"). How does he achieve his dream in spite of initial failure and the unexpected challenges nature throws at him? How does accomplishing this impossible task give his life meaning?

Man vs. society

Our protagonist struggles between deciding which is more fulfilling – a contemplative life or one of the flesh. How does society pull him toward one of the flesh? In following the ways of society, how much of his individuality must he give up?

Man vs. God(s)

Can material success in life guarantee anything about one's soul? What if a man believes it will only to find that it may not? Why would he initially believe it does (perhaps he views wealth as God's blessing for his character)? How does he come to the realization that material wealth may not equal salvation, and how does this affect his views on life's purpose and meaning?

Man vs. himself

What if our main character resists learning the purpose of his life because he is afraid to know the truth?

Why is he fearful of this? What forces compel him to learn the truth and to face the real nature of existence?

Guilt

Man vs. man

Our main character doesn't want to help someone he has responsibility for but at the same time feels guilt over his feelings of resentment or disinterest. How does he cope with the person who needs help, and how does he resolve his issues of guilt?

Man vs. society

The hero when a younger man committed a vile act, on behalf of his organization/government, and he has felt guilt about it for years. He's been able to suppress the shame, but one day another young man he knows (maybe someone he has trained) is asked to commit the same atrocity. How does our hero prevent this young man from doing so, and how does he survive bucking a system that cares little for his individual psyche?

Man vs. God(s)

What if our protagonist comes to believe that the faith he grew up in causes his guilt and shame rather than offering him solace from it? What event (perhaps a sin?) precipitated this belief? How does he struggle with those of his faith and God, and how does he ultimately resolve his conflict with them?

Man vs. himself

The main character, dealing with personal guilt for a bad, injurious choice he once made, finds a victim of a crime paralleling his. The discovery of this victim makes his guilt so unbearable that he must atone for it to set his world right. How does he go about coping with his guilt and making it right so he can live with himself?

Hope

Man vs. nature

What are the traits and qualities that allow hope to flourish? Courage? Faith? Ingenuity? Resourcefulness? Trust? Determination? Have your main character survive a natural disaster and its aftermath, examining along the way how he maintains hope with those or other virtues.

Man vs. man

Two people find themselves in an extremely difficult situation involving both of them. One character begins to succumb to pessimism while the other holds on to hopefulness. How does the latter character instill hope in his pessimistic counterpart so they can survive their situation?

Man vs. society

What if to escape a horrible situation or to avoid a devastating calamity, the only viable solution seems counterintuitive – and is the one our main character cannot convince others to get behind? How does he persuade a people without hope that there is a way out and that the solution will work?

Man vs. himself

What if the protagonist becomes a spent force, unable to fulfill his duties and responsibilities? How did he become this way? How does he gain hope rather than fall deeper into dark pessimism and depression?

Identity

Man vs. nature

Your main character is stuck in a perilous environment in which he comes to question all he believes in, as he barely is able to survive his journey to safety. What new virtues does he come to cherish, and how does he come to define himself, as he slowly, achingly, closes on a successful conclusion of his journey?

Man vs. man

A person with amnesia arrives at the main character's doorstep. How does our main character help him find his way in the world? How does the main character search to determine the amnesia victim's identity? What if this victim doesn't want to learn who he is?

Man vs. society

Our main character finds himself stuck in a place where he is unable to communicate with others. How does he find his way? What if this society looks down upon him because of his inability to communicate?

Man vs. himself

The main character finds he is unable to settle on his own identity, which is exemplified in his constantly changing outward expression of self (haircut, facial expressions, clothing, favorite verbal expressions, etc.). How through self-examination does he determine what is meaningful to him? How in the end does he imagine his future so he can determine who he is today?

Inflexibility

Man vs. nature

An explorer of a great wilderness area refuses to give up the trappings of civilization/his military organization despite that it's hampering the journey. Why won't he give up his notions of civilization/hierarchy? Will his inflexibility ultimately doom him, given the wilderness' unyielding stressors?

Man vs. man

Our main character cannot understand why his spouse wants him to be something he isn't (or even wants to be). How does he handle his spouse's criticism, and what can he do to get his spouse to acknowledge his wants and needs?

Man vs. society

The main character – a younger man – wants to do something/go into a career that his parents and those around him in society – neighbors, former teachers, parents' coworkers, even his friends – object to. Will he cave to their pressure or become what he wants to be, even if it means being on his own?

Man vs. himself

Our main character discovers something about a loved one – perhaps his child – that he cannot forgive/accept. Why is he so inflexible? Can he find a way to accept his loved one, or will he live a life in which both suffer isolation from one another?

Innocence lost

Man vs. nature

While in the wilderness on a camping or backpacking trip, something occurs that causes our young main character to almost die and in the process to gain a broader awareness of evil in the world. Feeling the pain of this new awareness, how does he survive not only his only mental anguish but also the wilderness as he makes his way back to civilization?

Man vs. man

How do two people who feel guilt about the loss of their loved ones come to feel love for one another? Why do they feel this guilt? How do they overcome it? How do they come to understand that they are right for one another when they each think they've lost the love of their lives or the only one for them?

Man vs. society

What if our protagonist, to get out of a jam (maybe to pay off a gambling debt or to avoid bankruptcy) decides to strike a deal with the devil (perhaps a crime syndicate or a hard-nosed but wealthy employer) to cover him. How does this deal make his situation worse for him? How does he extricate himself from it?

Man vs. himself

Our main character possesses special abilities that make him vital to solving a great crisis. Yet those abilities means he will be responsible for incredible – but seemingly inevitable – atrocities. How does he come to grips with the clear consequences of his growing abilities, as they are honed for solving the great crisis?

Isolation

Man vs. nature

A disaster leaves the main character stranded a long way from civilization. With little hope of rescue, he decides living alone and isolated is worth the risk of a perilous journey back to where he came. How does he succeed at overcoming the challenges nature throws at him?

Man vs. man

What if two people fall for each other but when the other isn't ready for a relationship? How do they maintain their "friendship" through all of this? What do they learn about themselves from their series of near-misses? What motivates them to keep trying over and over? Can they ever come together into a relationship by story's end?

Man vs. society

A man loses his job (or perhaps his wife leaves him), but to avoid his neighbors' shunning, begins a charade that he is still employed (or that the wife is still living there). Why does he believe his neighbors would shun him? What if others begin to suspect he's lying? Does he ever reveal the truth about his situation?

Man vs. himself

What if our main character, who fears being isolated and alone, keeps getting himself into toxic relationships in which his self-worth actually is diminished?

How does he come to feel even more isolated and alone in these relationships? How will he come to realize that true freedom, personal value, and love will come only when he lets go of his fear of being alone?

Jealousy

Man vs. nature

What if the antagonist's jealousy leads him to banish a loved one to a wilderness? How does he overcome the natural dangers of this exile? What does he learn from this that allows him to first survive then thrive?

Man vs. man

The protagonist discovers his best friend is dating the woman he's always longed for from afar. Overcome with jealousy, he competes with his best friend for the heart of this woman. How does he do that? Who will the woman decide is the better man (if either one!)?

Man vs. society

Our main character is jealous of others in an organization he belongs to or a company he works for. He believes they are wealthier, better traveled, more cultured than he is. He decides to prove he is second to none, but there are those he envies who wish to keep him in his place. How does he deal with them – and with his inner demons?

Man vs. himself

Our main character finds that his divorced ex is now happy with a new man. Rather than be angry at her, he is jealous of the new man, especially in light that he has lost everything he knew himself to be – a married man, a father who saw his children every day, his nice home and earnings. How does he overcome this jealousy before it eats him from the inside out, destroying what little he has left?

Loneliness

Man vs. nature

What if a man is stranded by himself on an island, in the deep jungle or on an alien planet? How does he survive the unforgiving environment only to find his greatest challenge may be his own loneliness?

Man vs. society

Our main character constantly senses he is different from others, and this leads to deep feelings of loneliness. What happens when he tries to determine why he is different – is there some great secret about him (or about human existence) that can be revealed?

Man vs. God(s)

What if the main character is driven by a loneliness that money and material goods can't salve? Why is he resistant to embracing the spiritual? How does he ultimately decide to at least explore the spiritual (and find that it at least partially alleviates loneliness)?

Man vs. himself

The protagonist is helping a woman raise her child (which is not his). One day, his true love from the past returns. What arguments go through his head for staying and for taking off with his old love? Perhaps the protagonist feels that he's always been the one who gives but never receives or makes a decisions that are for himself. What decision does he make?

Loss

Man vs. nature

During an expedition, a calamity occurs, cutting off our main character from most of his party. How does he survive and overcome the challenges of nature as trying to reunite with the main group?

Man vs. man

What if our main character has taken care of someone special (perhaps a foster child, an orphan, etc.) for a period of time and one day a person comes along to claim that special someone? How does our main character stop this new person from taking that special someone?

Man vs. society

Our main character finds he suffers from a spiritual emptiness that broader society seems to encourage because of its declining ethical behavior. In a decadent society, how does he lead a life based on his deeply-held moral values?

Man vs. himself

The protagonist is in a healing profession – probably psychology – but despite his success with others finds that he is unable to heal his own broken heart. What is needed for him to heal? Perhaps the one patient he seems unable to help?

Manipulation

Man vs. nature

An expedition is marooned in a remote wilderness. Each effort the protagonist and his expedition makes to overcome the challenges nature poses to their survival is undercut, however. What if their efforts were being manipulated to doom them? How do they determine this, and how do they discover who is sabotaging them?

Man vs. man

Two brothers vie for something – control of a family fortune, a throne, their father's affection. What happens when their zeal for achieving mastery over the other causes them to manipulate people? How many will be hurt by their manipulation? Can anyone end their game?

Man vs. society

What if an organization with evil intent attempts to manipulate our protagonist into committing a murder? How do they go about doing this? How does our main character come to suspect he is being manipulated, and how does he go about turning the tables on this organization?

Man vs. himself

Manipulation typically involves telling lies about oneself and others. What happens to the manipulator when he has told so many lies that he begins to believe them himself? Is there any way out of his internal madness and the life he has created?

Masquerade

Man vs. nature

The main character takes the place of another person (perhaps by pretending to be him) to ensure the latter is not captured or placed in a difficult situation. Our hero escapes but is ill-equipped to survive the wilderness he must make his way through (as eluding his former captors) to return home. What virtues does our hero possess that allows him to succeed?

Man vs. man

A new neighbor acts mysteriously, and our main character investigates. What secret does our main character discover? What does the neighbor do upon discoering he's being investigated and when his secret is found out?

Man vs. society

A family is falling apart, as each member – perhaps one suffers from alcohol addiction, perhaps another is dealing with a forced reduction in pay during a company downsizing, perhaps another is seeing a therapist for depression – fights with one another. If there's one thing they all agree upon, though, it's that their problems and disagreements must be kept secret from others. Can such a façade be maintained, or is it the catalyst of their undoing?

Man vs. himself

Your main character, caught up in the events of some

war, is coerced into committing an atrocity. Years later, how does he deal with his personal guilt for those horrors while at the same time keeping his culpability secret from others?

Memory

Man vs. man

What if the main character's memory of a lost spouse or lover drives a wedge between himself and a new woman in his life, a woman who loves him very much? How does their relationship unravel because of this? Can it be sewed back up?

Man vs. society

To avenge a great wrong, the protagonist must make a deal with the devil and commit some atrocious act (perhaps for information or materials so the revenge can be carried out). Can the protagonist fake the atrocious act or will he decide the price for silencing the memories torturing him is too great?

Man vs. God(s)

What if a man is asked to explain why he has no remorse for a terrible crime he committed? Would the the way he lost his sense of guilt and regret involve losing his faith? As he recalls what occurred, weave between these two developments in his view of life.

Man vs. himself

Our main character wakes up and realizes he doesn't know who he is or where he's from. He does sense that someone is after him, though. How does he figure out who he is? Who is after him and for what person? How did he lose his memory? And how does he triumph over the person who's after him?

Misconception

Man vs. nature

A person important to our main character is accused of committing a horrible crime. To clear his name, our main character must find and bring back evidence located in a dangerous wilderness. How does our main character overcome the challenges of nature to find this evidence? And what if someone is intent on ensuring he doesn't survive those dangers? What is the antagonist's motivation?

Man vs. man

What if our protagonist falls in love with a woman who has a notorious reputation – but he thinks it is merely a façade she has created? Why does he think it is merely a façade? And what if once he's in too deep there are hints that she really is using him? Can he see through her deceit?

Man vs. society

A false rumor or an outright lie has been told about our main character. Before our protagonist knows it, the rumor/lie affects his ability to function in his neighborhood/job. How does he deal with the rumor/lie, especially when he finds that there is evidence to support these untruths?

Man vs. himself

What if our main character has made every right decision in life, leading him to incredible success in his

career, finances and reputation – then one day he
wakes up and realizes that it all had been a grave mis-
calculation for it never led to his happiness. Can he
reshape his life by making the right decisions – despite
enormous pressure not to – so he can find happiness?
How does he relearn how to live the life he really
wants to lead rather than the one he has created for
himself?

Mysterious gift

Man vs. man

As the main character attempts to find out why he received a mysterious gift, he learns that another person wants this item. What actions does this nemesis take to commandeer the gift? Why does the main character simply not give up the gift? What is the secret behind the gift?

Man vs. society

The main character possesses a wonderful talent – a "gift," as others in society term it – perhaps as a musician or an artist. What if the main character does not wish to express his gift as society wishes him to? Why does he want to act contrary to society's desires?

Man vs. God(s)

A gift comes in the form of a "miracle." What if the main character, though, doesn't see it as a miracle? What if this miracle is not enough to resolve a need, wish or prayer?

Man vs. himself

The main character possesses an ability – a "gift," as some view it – that he views as a terrible burden. In fact, the character doesn't want to use his gift. Why is this? And what if a crisis arises that only the main character can resolve by using his special ability?

Obsession

Man vs. nature
Obsessed with finding a treasure, our main character enters a perilous wilderness where he must fight off nature's challenges. How do each of the challenges alter him – do they deepen his obsession or cause his view of what is important in life to evolve?

Man vs. man
Two men are obsessed with the same woman. Each will do anything to prevent the other from obtaining the woman's affections (She loves them both.). Which one will be victorious (Perhaps it will be the one who realizes his inner flaw and changes his behavior, which the woman finds uberattractive.)?

Man vs. society
A man who was adopted is obsessed with identifying his biological father/mother. But what if some organization doesn't want that information to be known? Why not? How much will our main character risk to fulfill his dream...or is it his obsession?

Man vs. himself
What if our protagonist is obsessed with a woman who is seemingly perfect but holds dark secrets? What if he surreptitiously discovers what the secrets are and they're something he has trouble stomaching? Which wins out – his obsessive love for her or his inability to accept her for what she once did?

Out of one's league

Man vs. nature

The main character is on a jungle (or a mountain climbing) expedition that suffers a freak accident, leaving many in the party dead. How does the main character survive in an environment, in which he is out of his league, and get home? What virtues does he possess that ensures his survival? What lessons does he learn during his effort to survive?

Man vs. man

How does the main character win the heart of someone who is out of his league? What is his motivation for pursuing this person? What traits does he possess that actually makes him the right person for the one who is out of his league?

Man vs. society

How does one win a position – e.g. a job or political office – that is out of his league? Why does he want to obtain this position, though doing so appears hopeless?

Man vs. himself

Our protagonist must suppress his attraction for another person who is out of his league. But that other person keeps showing up in his life, making the rejection of his feelings difficult. How does he gain the confidence to reach out to this other person?

Perfection

Man vs. nature

What if our main character resides in a Garden of Eden-like setting – perhaps a perfectly-balanced living dome on another planet – but feels that it is like living in a cage? At what point does the perfectly balanced envir-onment, even if utterly beautiful, become sterile? What price does perfection carry? Can this perfect en-vironment symbolize utopian societies in general or some place on Earth?

Man vs. man

What if a married couple, who are our two main char-acters, realize they no longer love one another? Though feeling duped by society's promise that mar-riage meant happiness, they are unwilling to let go be-cause doing so means admitting their own failure and that the dream they staked their lives on was a mis-take. How do they come to terms with this, and along the way how do they seek happiness since they no longer can find it in one another?

Man vs. society

Our protagonist has a perfect physical appearance but finds that with this beauty come certain expectations from society that he doesn't feel is what's right for him. How does he balance others' perceptions and ex-pectations of him against who he really is and wants to be?

Man vs. himself

What if our main character finds himself bored by the perfection of his life, the kind of life that so many others would desire? After all, while there is no pain or suffering, there also is little joy or appreciation for anything. How does our main character break from this perfect world so that he can experience a meaningful life again?

Promise

Man vs. nature

A man makes a promise to his best friend (such as a soldier delivering a dying buddy's letter to a wife), but to keep it he must survive a difficult journey. What natural obstacles does he encounter along the way? In overcoming these obstacles, what does he learn that allows him to resolve an internal flaw that might prevent him from fulfilling his promise?

Man vs. man

A man has made a promise to another person then finds the antagonist is preventing him from keeping it. Why did he make this promise and why is keeping it so important? Why does the antagonist make fulfillment of this promise difficult? How does the man succeed despite this opposition?

Man vs. society

What if the very person the protagonist has promised to protect might just get him killed? Why did he make this promise? How can he convince the organization trying to capture/kill the person he's protecting to stop what it's doing?

Man vs. himself

The main character's loved one – who he's promised to marry – returns from service overseas. He finds his beloved's emotional scars from that experience and the new conflicts arising between them may be too much for him to keep his promise. What decision does he ultimately make about fulfilling his promise, and how does he arrive at it?

Race

Man vs. nature

The main character must accomplish a goal before an impending storm – say a hurricane or a blizzard – makes that impossible. What is the goal to be achieved and why is it so important? What happens when the main character, with his goal in reach, decides to keep pursuing it despite that the storm arrives?

Man vs. man

Our main character is engaged in a race with an old nemesis in which the winner will be able to prove his worth and gain something of great value. What struggles have the characters had in the past with one another? How might the nemesis underhandedly attempt to prevent the main character from winning?

Man vs. God(s)

What if the main character – angry at the world and angry at God – decides to enter a dangerous race that he may not be qualified to participate? How does this attempt to prove his anger is justified actually bring him closer to God? Why he is angry at the world and God in the first place?

Man vs. himself

Our protagonist has five minutes to disarm a bomb whose construction he's entirely unfamiliar with. How does he keep his cool and succeed?

Reclaim

Man vs. nature

To regain his birthright, our exiled main character must return to his land and reclaim it. Doing so, however, requires that he take on several challenges of nature – unfriendly environments, dangerous creatures. What do each of these challenges symbolize to show that our main character is worthy to recover his position (for example, tests of courage, endurance, intelligence, etc.)?

Man vs. man

The main character's daughter is kidnapped. Who would kidnap her and for what purpose? How does the main character first locate where she is being held and then rescue her? Perhaps he needs to draw favors upon a team of old companions whose lives are in disarray?

Man vs. society

Our protagonist is sent to retrieve a device that would provide its holder with great power. How does he locate this device, and what if he decides, upon learning about its full potential, that no one should have it? How does he keep the device from the very people who hired him to recover it?

Man vs. himself

Your main character has suffered a serious accident. How does he recover from it, even though he may never be able to fully lead the life he once led? How does he handle his self-doubts?

Removal

Man vs. nature

What if your main character were sent to capture or destroy some beast in the wilderness – a challenging task for sure, yet one he is well-suited for handling – but the creature turns out to be something more terrifying and powerful than he initially was led to believe? How does he defeat this beast? To make this more than a run-of-the-mill science fiction or fantasy tale, can the beast symbolize some element of society that our hero must metaphorically tame and subjugate?

Man vs. man

The main character needs to get rid of someone, such as an unwanted roommate or an annoying coworker. What is the motivation for doing this? How does he achieve this goal despite his opponent's efforts to thwart him?

Man vs. society

Your main character needs to get rid of a new company/venture that has come to town or perhaps to unveil the unjust actions of a prominent family in town – both are popular with the locals, however. Why does he want to get rid of this new business/respected family? How does he change the minds of the townsfolk?

Man vs. himself

To fill his inner emptiness, our main character engages

in a life of decadence – parties, alcohol or drugs, indis-criminate sex – and with increasing speed it's spinning out of control. Our main character begins to sense this but finds the distraction at least a temporary relief. How does he regain control of his life and address the inner emptiness that actually even further consumes him, as he falls deeper into the pit of decadence? Can he ever remove himself from it?

Resistance

Man vs. nature

Our protagonist is ordered to secretly escort an important dignitary through an extremely dangerous terrain. What challenges of nature must the protagonist overcome to accomplish his mission? What if the greatest obstacle he faces is a human conspiracy involving the dignitary?

Man vs. man

How does our main character deny an attraction that he and another character, who is a real mismatch, feel for one another? Why are they mismatched? What do they find attractive about one another? How do they resist this attraction? How do they ultimately come together?

Man vs. society

What if two characters form a bond with one another despite their disparate backgrounds? Why and how does this bond form? What resistance does this connection face from society? How do they ensure their bond survives in spite of the prevailing, prejudiced culture?

Man vs. himself

Is the power of passion greater than the force of expectation? What if our protagonist must decide between his personal desire for freedom and what her family/culture require of him? Which will he choose?

Returning

Man vs. nature
The protagonist's ship crashes on a planet so that he has no way to return home. How does he survive until a rescue can be mounted?

Man vs. man
Our main character's spouse is away for an extended period on an important assignment. During that time, the main character – though helping to support his spouse – falls in love with another person who is doing the same for her spouse. What happens when the spouses return? Can the main character and his new beloved leave one another?

Man vs. society
The main character returns home after several years of being away but is not particularly welcomed by his family. Why did he leave in the first place? What compelled him to return home? How does he find acceptance from his estranged family?

Man vs. himself
A man loses his hearing or goes blind. Doctors say it may be temporary. "May" is the operative word. How does the man cope with the possibility that his loss might be permanent? What is the balance between hope and being realistic?

Revenge

Man vs. nature

While on a trip in the wilderness to rest and relax, our main character finds that someone is out to kill him for revenge. How does he survive the challenges of nature as trying to outwit his would-be assassin?

Man vs. man

The main character's former spouse, livid at her perceived abandonment and betrayal, plots to send him to prison and ruin his life. How would she do this? What effect would this have on the main character's friendships, career and intimate relationships? How would the main character respond to and overcome this threat?

Man vs. society

What if to destroy the society that suppresses his people, the protagonist must become one of his overlords (Perhaps through an elaborate scheme he infiltrates this society.)? Will the material trappings of the suppressor become too much for him to resist? How does he go about bringing the collapse of this society? What if a member of the suppressor discovers his secret plan?

Man vs. himself

Our protagonist must decide if he will avenge a man who stole his wife after ripping apart his family and life. On one level, the protagonist may fantasize about revenge and decide there's nothing that can be done in the real world. On another level, he may be overcome with emotion and act out of passion. Or perhaps he will realize that no one stole his wife but that he lost it all on his own and make changes to ensure this doesn't happen to him again. What choice will he make, and how will he arrive at it?

Sanity

Man vs. nature

Our protagonist believes that a place he must regularly pass through somehow is malevolent. Why does he believe this? As he falls deeper and deeper into his neurosis and insanity, how does he try to climb back out? Is there any way out? Can the evil place be symbolic of some abstract concept that many in our society suffer a deep neurosis about?

Man vs. man

How does someone maintain his sanity when abused by another? What is his personal story of surviving a living hell? What psychological trauma does he suffer afterward?

Man vs. society

Our main character finds himself thrust into a shadowy underworld where people's behavior appears to be irrational, even insane. How does he tease out the logic in their seedy behavior and manipulate it so he can return to his own sane, rational world? What if upon returning he finds that his world is just as mad as the one he left?

Man vs. himself

What if our main character begins to witness signs of paranormal activity that no one else can see? How does he discover if these strange events are "real" – and how does he maintain his sanity?

Secrecy

Man vs. nature

The main character is sent on a quest to find some object. Where the object is held, though, is a secret. To locate it, he must cross a number of dangerous environments with which he is unfamiliar. How does he survive these natural hazards and find the object?

Man vs. man

Our main character discovers a shocking secret about a loved one. What is the secret? How does he verify it? What is ambiguous about some of the facts that would seem to verify it? How does knowing this secret change his perspective about his loved one and his own life?

Man vs. society

Our protagonist has a special ability that she must keep secret from society. What is this ability, and why must she keep it hidden? How does she go about keeping it secret? What if one day, through an accidental slip, she reveals her secret and others (maybe the government) come after her so they can use her secret skills for their purposes?

Man vs. himself

The main character is uncomfortable with his family's legacy and so attempts to run from it. What is this legacy? How does he attempt to hide it? Can a man ever truly run away from something that is an internal problem he must come to terms with?

Separation

Man vs. nature

Two men on an expedition become separated thanks to a freak accident. To survive, however, each needs the other – the share of the gear they carry, their expertise, their companionship. How do our two characters overcome the challenges nature throws at them as they attempt to reunite? What can each man learn about themselves and perhaps each other as they overcome these difficulties?

Man vs. man

Our protagonist finds he has difficultly connecting with others, which leads him to the edge of serious mental and physical health issues. Why is he unable to connect? What steps does he take try to connect? Are some people, by their very nature, unable to connect with others?

Man vs. society

The main character is separated from a loved one. How did they become separated? Why is this separation so unbearable? How do the two characters attempt to reunite? What obstacles do various elements of society throw at them to prevent them from seeing one another?

Man vs. himself

Our main character loses something of great importance to him – a position of prestige, a loved one, maybe both. How does he regain his sense of identity and self-worth in the aftermath of such a loss? How did he lose what he so much needed and loved?

Tracked

Man vs. nature

Your main character is hired to kill a creature – a dangerous escaped animal, a monster of some sort, an alien beast. How does the main character go about capturing it? Elevate the power of this story by having the main character discover something about the creature that leads him to believe it should not be captured.

Man vs. man

The main character is tasked with capturing someone – a man wanted for a crime, an escaped convict, someone who holds a dark secret. How does our main character go about finding this person? What lessons about himself does the main character learn as he fails through the story's rising action to capture the person?

Man vs. society

What if your main character is wanted by law enforcement or an intelligence agency? What is he wanted for? How does he avoid being caught by that organization? What does he learn about himself as the organization closes on his capture?

Man vs. himself

What if your main character, whose job is to track down someone, uncovers clues about the hunted that leads him to doubt his assignment? Focus on his internal struggle to rectify his assignment against his morals and the truth.

Trapped

Man vs. nature

A man alone in the wilds is trapped by a freak accident – e.g. pinned down in an avalanche, cut off by a flash-flood or a forest fire, stuck atop a mountain ledge because his climbing rope has broke. How does he survive nature's elements until help can – if it ever will – arrive?

Man vs. man

Our main character is kidnapped for ransom. How does he survive his captivity? Why was he kidnapped and by whom? Can he ultimately escape by psychologically working over one of his keepers?

Man vs. society

A person trapped by circumstances but who desires more – romance, glamour, fun – finds himself at odds with his family's values. How can he escape his circumstances, if only temporarily? Must he ultimately sacrifice a relationship with his family to obtain freedom?

Man vs. himself

After a disaster occurs, our protagonist finds himself alone. While he probably can survive for years where he is despite the calamity, he knows there is no way to escape, nil chance of being rescued for at least several months, and that he is entirely by himself. How does he maintain his sanity until rescue arrives?

Turning a new page

Man vs. nature

The main character decides that to become the person he wants to be, he must accept some new challenge in a foreboding environment that he is unfamiliar with (say moving from sunny Southern California to the Arctic). What obstacles in nature threaten his ability to complete the new challenge?

Man vs. man

What if after a life-changing event two people – maybe father and son, mother and daughter, or husband and wife – must create a new destiny together but find themselves at odds with one another about how to do so? Why do they have different dreams? How do they find a future together?

Man vs. society

After a calamitous event in the main character's life, he moves to another town where he plans to start a new chapter in his life by opening a running a business he's always dreamed of. The local residents aren't too keen on his new business or he coming to their town, though. How does he overcome the townsfolks' cool reception to him and succeed at his new business?

Man vs. self

The main character has an addiction that he knows needs to be overcome or his world will fall part – perhaps by losing his family, his career, his self-worth.

How does he overcome this addiction – as well as the personal demons of the past that haunt him and lead to the dependency?

Uncertainty

Man vs. man

The main character must determine if someone he loves truly shares the same feelings for him or is just manipulating him. What clues does he have of manipulation? Why would someone want to manipulate him (and what is at stake if he is)? How does he go about determining his beloved's true intentions?

Man vs. society

What if a man were told that the body of his father – who has been missing for some time – has been found? How does the man deal with this new information? What if the man suspects that the body really isn't that of his father – but when he tries to find the truth, there are forces that don't want him to know? What secrets are they keeping, how does his father play a part in them, and how did presenting a body they say is his help hide the truth?

Man vs. God(s)

What happens when our protagonist meets someone of a different theological persuasion, perhaps one that he even finds repulsive? What if this person then saves the protagonist's life? How does the protagonist question his own theological beliefs, and how does he rectify them given all that has occurred with "the enemy"?

Man vs. himself

The main character's loved one has a once-in-a-lifetime

opportunity, but our protagonist can't afford it. How does he cope with this inability? What steps does he take to find the money for this opportunity? Will these steps include breaking ethical rules and principles that the main character always has lived by and that his loved one admires in him?

Vengeance

Man vs. nature

In an act of revenge, a man sabotages a boat or a small plane, leaving his nemesis – our main character – stranded at sea or in an inhospitable environment. How does the main character survive nature's threats? Does he then seek revenge himself on the man who set him up to die?

Man vs. man

Desperate to lay his past to rest, the antagonist decides to exact revenge on all who made him miserable – including our story's protagonist. What can our protagonist do to stop the villain? Does the protagonist feel any guilt over what he did in the past to the antagonist? Why or why not?

Man vs. society

Our main character decides his hatred for the current system justifies supporting an invader who will wipe it out. But does support of the invader mean an even worse system will be ushered in? What if the main character determines after the invasion that it does – and then switches sides?

Man vs. himself

For a perceived injustice against those who the protagonist holds dear but was unable to fully protect, he decides to seek revenge. Why was he not able to protect those he loved? Can revenge bring redemption and justice or will it only bring more destruction, including of his own soul?

Violence

Man vs. man

Two characters are caught in a situation in which they are pitted against one another in some sort of savage competition. Why are they set against one another? What if one of them decides to no longer fight? How does he convince the other to not fight?

Man vs. society

Our main character lives in a setting where violence is rampant. What if he decides he no longer can abide being violent as well? How does he arrive at this turning point? With such an attitude, can he survive long in this setting? How does he begin to encourage and change others to be nonviolent?

Man vs. God(s)

A man suffers during horrific acts of violence (e.g. genocide, a political purge in a third world country, revenge by a drug cartel) that causes him to question God's existence; after all, how could a just God allow such horrors to occur? How does he regain his faith? Perhaps he discovers that without faith, he increasingly behaves in the same ways that those who caused him so much pain?

Man vs. himself

The protagonist finds himself in a situation (e.g. an occupying army, a gang, prison) where depravity involving violence is the norm. Unable to walk away from it, how does his conscience wrestle with the horrors he witnesses and even is expected to participate in?

Wrongly accused

Man vs. nature

Falsely accused by his closest friends, a man is abandoned or imprisoned in a hostile wilderness. How does he escape/survive Mother Nature and upon returning to civilization prove his innocence? Or will he be bent on revenge? Why did his friends betray him?

Man vs. man

Two former lovers are coincidentally trapped together. To survive, they must work together and confront the other about their shared past in which each (wrongly) believe the other guilty of some betrayal. What circumstances caused them to be trapped, and can this be symbolic of the emotional trap they've been in since their breakup? How do they ultimately come to be lovers (or at least friends) again?

Man vs. society

A person who generally is considered virtuous is arrested. What he is arrested for? Was the arrest part of some conspiracy? How does he prove his innocence?

Man vs. himself

Our protagonist suffers a terrible fate because he has been wrongly accused. Can he ever forgive his accusers? How does he learn that the only way to inner peace given his situation is to make peace with those who have hurt him?

Zealotry

Man vs. nature
What if to undergo a rite of passage our young protag-onist must spend time alone in the wilderness? How does he survive when he is ill prepared to? How does the experience affect his views of the zealots who re-quired this rite and of the views they espouse?

Man vs. man
Our protagonist learns of an assassination plot, but no one takes him seriously, so he takes it upon himself to foil a zealot's plans. How does he do this? Why do those in charge not take him seriously, and how do they ac-tually hinder him from stopping the assassination?

Man vs. society
Our main character commits some seemingly harmless act that makes him the target of zealots. How does he avoid being killed by them? Is there any way he can ever end this situation, given that every zealot he stops becomes a martyr inspiring others to come after him?

Man vs. God(s)
The main character begins a journey that ultimately causes him to be an ambassador of some faith. What if this is a journey that he is reluctant to take? Why would he be reluctant? And what event(s) set this journey in motion and took him along for the ride, though he wishes he could get off the boat?

Create Your Own Prompts

Good stories center on the clashing of characters' goals and motivations. If trying to come up with a compelling story idea, as you go through your day think of situations in which characters can come into conflict with one another.

Here are three such areas you can mine for story ideas.

Scour the news

Headlines are a source of great stories. Always ask "what if" in conjunction with the headline and then build the story from there: "Boat capsizes, leaving 115 dead" – but what if there were 116 passengers? What happened to the one who survived? How did he survive? Ask "What is the real story?" Why did that boat capsize? Did it carry a spy or someone with information who needed to "disappear"? Was it revenge for not paying up to the local mob?

Add a family member

Usually in happy families, each member has found a

satisfying position or role in it. Think about the different people you pass each day and disrupt this happy
family by adding one of them as a new member. For
example, what if siblings discovered that their father
had a child with another woman than their mother?
What if a single mother out of the blue marries a man,
giving her children a stepfather? What if half-siblings
suddenly come to live with a remarried man and his
wife and children? How must each character change so
that happiness can be restored?

Enter a portal

Symbolically, going through a door, turnstile, window
or other opening is an entryway into another world.
Look for such portals during your day and ask what
would happen if your main character passes through a
portal in which he shouldn't go – a desperately poor
mother into a store with an open but unattended cash
register, an escaped slave on a train heading west, a
custodian into a scientist's experimental wormhole?
How does entering this portal change your main character's life? What obstacles does your main character
face in this new world? Would the main character want
to stay there?

About the Author

Rob Bignell is the owner and chief editor of Inventing Reality Editing Service, which meets the editing and proofreading needs of writers both new and published. Several of his short stories in the literary and science fiction genres have been published, and he is the author of the literary novel "Windmill", the nonfiction "7 Minutes a Day...", "Best Sights to See", "Hikes with Tykes", "Headin' to the Cabin", and "Hittin' the Trail" guidebooks, and the poetry collection "Love Letters to Sophie's Mom." For more than two decades, he worked as an award-winning journalist, with half of those years spent as an editor. He spent another seven years as an English teacher and community college journalism instructor. He holds a Master's degree in English and a Bachelor's in journalism and English.

CHECK OUT THESE OTHER GREAT WRITING GUIDEBOOKS BY THE AUTHOR

➢ **7 Minutes a Day to Your Bestseller** – Novel writers receive expert advice on topics like motivating yourself to write, starting your story with exciting opening lines, creating intriguing characters, mastering the craft of writing to elevate your style, and pitching your story to potential publishers.

➢ **7 Minutes a Day to a Self-Published Book** – Whether writing a novel or nonfiction, whether planning to print a paperback or an ebook, this book guides you through the self-publishing process, from the title page to the index, from designing a cover to formatting your text.

➢ **7 Minutes a Day to Promoting Your Book** – You'll develop a strategy that will get articles about your self-published book in newspapers, magazines, on radio and television programs, posted on blogs, and linked to on websites, while landing you book signings and readings, all at virtually no cost.

➢ **7 Minutes a Day to Mastering the Craft of Writing** – Craft is as important to storytelling as the plot or characters. This book gives you 50 tried-and-true techniques to improve your writing craftsmanship, including using active voice, showing not telling, ramping up dramatic tension, and being more descriptive.

➢ **Writing Affirmations: A Collection of Positive Messages to Inspire Writers** – Suffering from writer's block? Self-doubt about your talent? Has creative writing lost its joy? You can reclaim the pleasure of writing and pen the book you've always dreamed of. Respected and award-winning author Rob Bignell offers uplifting, meaningful phrases that can be read out loud or internalized weekly over the course of a year. Writing prompts and tips follow each affirmation, giving you the inspiration and motivation to keep writing.

NEED
AN EDITOR?

Having your book, business document or
academic paper proofread or edited before
submitting it can prove invaluable. In an
economic climate where you face heavy
competition, your writing needs a second eye
to give you the edge. The author of this title and
the "7 Minutes a Day…" writing guidebook
series can provide that second eye.

FIND OUT MORE AT:
https://inventingrealityediting.
wordpress.com/home

www.ingramcontent.com/pod-product-compliance
Lightning Source LLC
Chambersburg PA
CBHW050546280326
41933CB00011B/1737